PUFFIN BOOKS

Poetry Jump-Up

Grace Nichols was born in Guyana and came to Britain in 1977. In 1983 she won the Commonwealth Poetry Prize for her cycle of poems, *i is a long memoried woman.* She is the author of several books for children and now lives in Sussex.

Other poetry books by Grace Nichols

GIVE YOURSELF A HUG

For younger readers

NO HICKORY, NO DICKORY, NO DOCK
(with John Agard)

Compiled by Grace Nichols

Poetry Jump-Up

Illustrated by Michael Lewis

PUFFIN BOOKS

PUFFIN BOOKS

Published by the Penguin Group
Penguin Books Ltd, 27 Wrights Lane, London W8 5TZ, England
Penguin Putnam Inc., 375 Hudson Street, New York, New York 10014, USA
Penguin Books Australia Ltd, Ringwood, Victoria, Australia
Penguin Books Canada Ltd, 10 Alcorn Avenue, Toronto, Ontario, Canada M4V 3B2
Penguin Books India (P) Ltd, 11 Community Centre, Panchsheel Park,
New Delhi – 110 017, India
Penguin Books (NZ) Ltd, Cnr Rosedale and Airborne Roads, Albany, Auckland, New Zealand
Penguin Books (South Africa) (Pty) Ltd, 5 Watkins Street, Denver Ext 4,
Johannesburg 2094, South Africa

On the World Wide Web at: www.penguin.com

Penguin Books Ltd, Registered Offices: Harmondsworth, Middlesex, England

This collection first published by Blackie and Son Ltd as *Black Poetry* 1988
Published in Puffin Books 1990
10

Made and printed in England by Clays Ltd, St Ives plc

British Library Cataloguing in Publication Data
A CIP catalogue record for this book is available from the British Library

ISBN 0-140-34053-X

Contents

Foreword   7

The Beauty Of It   11

Kid Stuff   27

Poor Fowl and Other Creatures   49

Hard Times/Work Times   63

Way Down in the Music   83

Magic and Old Days   95

A Taste of Asia   115

Index of First Lines   138

Acknowledgements   141

Some would argue that poetry has no colour and that one wouldn't dream of putting together an anthology of 'white poetry'. One might well say as a parallel to this, that the fact that one wouldn't need to describe an anthology of poems by men as 'men's poetry' as opposed to 'women's poetry' points to certain real issues of omission and neglect by the literary establishment and to the whole question of power.

When I was approached about putting together this collection of poems for children by 'black poets' I was enormously excited by the idea. I saw this as a way of offering children something new; new sounds and tastes and ways with words. I think it's important for all children (black or white) to be exposed to poetry from different cultures and to be aware that black poets exist and contribute to the world's literary heritage.

But putting the anthology together was no straightforward undertaking. While poets such as Dionne Brand, Eloise Greenfield, John Agard, Nikki Giovanni and myself have produced collections for young children, a number of good black poets just happen to have work that is geared to adults. And apart from the rummaging and unearthing and waiting on poets who promised 'a new one', I found myself having to deal with the controversy surrounding the term 'black' itself.

Black evokes for me, almost unconsciously, a certain cultural spirit or aesthetic with underlying connections to an African past. This spirit manifests itself in the creole speech of the Caribbean for example; in the black English of Afro-Americans; in the blues, jazz, gospel, calypso and dub, the influences of which can be felt on Afro-American and Caribbean poetry.

7

At the same time, however, I'm aware of the broader 'political colour' of the term black which extends to include Asians who also find themselves discriminated against because of their colour. I'm also aware that some Asians object to the term 'black' and see it as a blanket label, denying their own distinctive identity. Discussions go on as to whether black should be seen as a racial/cultural definition or should be seen as a political definition for people of colour who've shared a common resistance to discrimination.

Certainly, in the case of the Caribbean, if the definition of race were applied exclusively, poets like Ian McDonald, a white West Indian, and David Dabydeen, an East-Indian Guyanese, would have been omitted. Yet their work is very much rooted in the Caribbean.

Among the Asian poets I did not find many poems for children. But from the adult works of poets like Nissim Ezekiel, Eunice de Souza, Cecil Rajendra and A.K. Ramanujan, I selected what I felt could work for children. But this anthology is by no means a definitive one. As the poems weren't many and had their own kind of sensibility, I decided to have them grouped together in a section of their own rather than have them lost away in the overall collection.

I've had great pleasure in putting this anthology together— a celebration of voices from the Caribbean, Afro-America, Asia, Africa and Britain. There was the great sense of discovery whenever I came across a new poem; the fun and warmth I had reading them, not to mention the poignancy, aroused by poems such as 'My Country' written by Mandela's daughter, then aged twelve.

Finally it is my hope (in fact I have little doubt) that children will skip this introduction and move straight into the poems, which are intended for them.

Grace Nichols

Lullaby

A heart to hate you
Is as far away as the moon.
A heart to love you
Is as close as the door.

Barundi

The Beauty Of It

I have often wondered
        about the beauty of its
                        darkness
tall
short
at ninety degrees angle
                    to my right
                        left
                        at my rear,
                        (keeping watch)
                        in front,
                        (running away)
with the sun as its lover
I have often wondered
            about the beauty of its
                    darkness,
my Shadow.

Don L. Lee

Wind

I pulled a hummingbird out of the sky one day
    but let it go,
I heard a song and carried it with me
    on my cotton streamers,
I dropped it on an ocean and lifted up a wave
    with my bare hands,
I made a whole canefield tremble and bend
    as I ran by,
I pushed a soft cloud from here to there,
I hurried a stream along a pebbled path,
I scooped up a yard of dirt and hurled it in the air,
I lifted a straw hat and sent it flying,
I broke a limb from a guava tree,
I became a breeze, bored and tired,
and hovered and hung and rustled and lay
    where I could.

Dionne Brand

Once the Wind

Once the wind
said to the sea
I am sad
        And the sea said
Why
        And the wind said
Because I
am not blue like the sky
or like you

        So the sea said what's
so sad about that
                Lots
of things are blue
or red or other colours too
        but nothing
neither sea nor sky
can blow so strong
or sing so long as you

        And the sea looked sad
         So the wind said
Why

Shake Keane

Knoxville, Tennessee

I always like summer
best
you can eat fresh corn
from daddy's garden
and okra
and greens
and cabbage
and lots of
barbecue
and buttermilk
and homemade ice-cream
at the church picnic
and listen to
gospel music
outside
at the church
homecoming
and go to the mountain with
your grandmother
and go barefooted
and be warm
all the time
not only when you go to bed
and sleep

Nikki Giovanni

I love me mudder . . .

I love me mudder and me mudder love me
we come so far from over de sea,
we heard dat de streets were paved with gold
sometime it hot sometime it cold
I love me mudder and me mudder love me
we try fe live in harmony
you might know her as Valerie
but to me she is my mummy.

She shouts at me daddy so loud some time
she don't smoke weed she don't drink wine
she always do the best she can
she work damn hard down ina England,
she's always singing some kind of song
she have big muscles and she very very strong
she likes pussy cats and she love cashew nuts
she don't bother with no if and buts.

I love me mudder and me mudder love me
we come so far from over de sea
we heard dat de streets were paved with gold
sometime it hot sometime it cold,
I love her and she love me too
and dis is a love I know is true
me and my mudder we love you too.

Benjamin Zephaniah

Reasons Why

Just because I loves you—
That's de reason why
Ma soul is full of color
Like de wings of a butterfly.

Just because I loves you
That's de reason why
Ma heart's a fluttering aspen leaf
When you pass by.

Langston Hughes

Six O'Clock Feeling

You ever feel
dat 6 o'clock feeling
6 o'clock shadow falling
wrappin you up
meking you stop
an tink
bout all dese tings
God doin
6 o'clock bee calling
All dem tree
tekking strange, strange shape
an stan up
sharp! sharp! gainst dat sky
You know dem 6 o'clock colour
pink an orange an blue an purple an black

dat 6 o'clock feeling
mekkin you feel like touchin
mekkin you feel so small
you could cry
or fall down pun you knee
and thank God
you could still
see He 6 o'clock sky

Kamal Singh

Dread-lock Style

Me don't want no hair style
cause me don't want no hair pile
pon me bedroom floor

I say me don't want no hair style
cause me don't want no hair pile
pon me bedroom floor

I think I gonna stick to me
dread-lock style
me dread-lock style
looking wild wild wild

dem hair gals
putting a dunno what on yuh hair
bunning up yuh scalp
thinking I was born yesterday

So I think I gonna stick
to me dread-lock style
me dread-lock style
looking wild wild wild

Lesley Miranda

For My Son

The street is in darkness
Children are sleeping
Mankind is dreaming
It is midnight.

It is midnight
The sun is away
Stars peep at cradles
Far seems the day.

Who will awaken
One little flower
Sleeping and growing
Hour and hour?

Light will awaken
All the young flowers
Sleeping and growing
Hour and hour.

Dew is awake
Morning is soon
Mankind is risen
Flowers will bloom.

Martin Carter

Watching the Sun

i wake to a yellow fire
a blazing light hanging
on my face
like a dream of floating balloons
dancing on my nose
& thru the wooden slats of jalousies
i see the leaves
of the mango tree playing
from fresh caresses of the wind
& in the sky
a dizzying blueness
that makes me want to sleep

i wake to a yellow fire
a blazing light hanging
on my face
whistles of keskidees
gently bringing me to life
& sounds of footsteps
like the charm of water-falls
to this smell of fried bakes
& salt-fish

& this yellow fire of dream
turns into the smiling face
of my mother

Amon Saba Saakana

The Friday Night Smell

I love the
friday night
smell of
mammie baking
bread—creeping
up to me in
bed, and tho
zzzz I'll fall
asleep, before i
even get a
bite—when
morning come,
you can bet
I'll meet a
kitchen table
laden with
bread, still
warm and fresh
salt bread
sweet bread
crisp and brown
& best of all
coconut buns
THAT's why
I love the
friday night
smell of mammie
baking bread
putting me to

sleep, dreaming
of jumping from
the highest branch
of the jamoon tree
into the red water
creek
beating carlton
run & catching
the biggest fish
in the world
plus, getting
the answers right
to every single
sum
that every day
in my dream
begins and ends
with the friday
night smell of
mammie baking
bread, and
coconut buns
of course.

Marc Matthews

Fruit in a Bowl

Fruit in a bowl.

Full goldenapples with veined skins so fine
That just a look might burst them –

                                    tangerines
For all the world like small green solid bells
Promising little kisses of astringency.

Yellow bananas, cool and firm to feel
Lying in curves of silken-tongued delight.

And great plumpted mangoes, sweetness
    to the seed.
Huge cut pawpaws bearing dark-seedling cargoes.

And sapodillas with their sweet, brown kernels
Aching to change to sugar once again.

Tropical fruit.

A. J. Seymour

KID STUFF

Ringmarole: Puzzles for Children

Some folks can live while other die,
Some folks can laugh while other cry,
Some places are far some are nigh,
Some folks like cake and other pie,
There's a low for every high,
Sometimes I wonder why.

Well, there's a this for every that,
And there's a tit for every tat,
You got to sit before you've sat,
And there's a chit for every chat,
You got to spit before you've spat,
If that's not true I'll eat my hat.

If there's a crisis, well there's a cross,
And something found was something lost,
Some things are free while others cost,
Some ride a mule, some ride a hoss,
A rolling stone don't catch no moss,
You work for me, that makes me boss.

Some roads are crooked, some are straight,
Some don't eat much, some clean the plate,
Some folks are early and some are late,
Some get in soon while others wait,
You call it luck, I call it fate,
You go through cracks, I find the gate.

Some folks got hair, some wear a wig,
Some dance the waltz, some do a jig,
Some things zag and some things zig,
Some are little and some are big,
Some get it easy while others dig,
I got my cow, you got your pig.

Here is rain and there is dew,
Here am I and there are you,
You are one, we both make two.
There is old and there is new,
Some things we fry and some things stew,
I don't know, I wish I knew . . .

The land is dry, the river wet,
Some babies cry and others fret,
Some folks perspire while others sweat,
Some doors are open, others shet,
I feel the wind, ain't seen it yet,
Now just how silly can this get?

There's a smile for every frown,
If I'm a fool then you're a clown,
If this is up, then that is down,
If this is square, then that is round,
Some folks swim and others drown,
I know how crazy all this sounds!

Elma Stuckley

Don't Hit Your Sister

He hit me on the face, Mummy
so I hit him back

He hit me on the leg, Mummy
so I hit him back

He hit me on the back, Mummy
so I hit him back on the back

He hurlded me, Mummy
so I hurlded him back

He was the one who started it, Mummy
so I started it back.

Lesley Miranda

Georgetown Children

Under the soursop silver-leaf tree
The High School children play skip-and-free

Sun burning down like a fire ball
Watch the children before school call

Laugh in their gay time, laughter rich,
Jump the jack, bring marble pitch.

Black child, yellow child, brown child, white
They all the same if you looking right.

Pass by any schoolyard in Georgetown atall
And watch the children before school call.

Under the soursop silver-leaf tree
The High School children play skip-and-free

The biggest thing in life could be
Watching the children play skip-and-free.

Ian McDonald

A Funny Man

I know a man a very funny man
and he lives in Oumbout Street
and he plays a band
with pots, pans

Oh that man in Oumbout Street
he plays with his shoes
on his hands and gloves
on his feet

Oh that man in Oumbout Street
He plays with his gloves
on his feet and shoes
on his hands as he
plays on his funny bands

Accabre Huntley

Granny Anna

I love my Granny Anna
Yes I love her so
For when I was little
She could never let me go

I care a lot about her
Like she does for me
When I'm with her I'm happy
And I always will be

I pray for her and hope that
She'll never die
And if she does I know she will
Watch me from the sky

Yansan Agard

Wha Me Mudder do

Mek me tell you wha me Mudder do
wha me mudder do
wha me mudder do

Me mudder pound plantain mek fufu
Me mudder catch crab mek calaloo stew

   Mek me tell you wha me mudder do
   wha me mudder do
   wha me mudder do

   Me mudder beat hammer
   Me mudder turn screw
   she paint chair red
   then she paint it blue

Mek me tell you wha me mudder do
wha me mudder do
wha me mudder do

Me mudder chase bad-cow
with one 'Shoo'
she paddle down river
in she own canoe
Ain't have nothing
dat me mudder can't do
Ain't have nothing
dat me mudder can't do

Mek me tell you

Grace Nichols

a heavy rap

i can run faster than any gazelle
last time i had a race i left him
on the inside corner of the indy 500
i can outswim any ole fish
gave a dolphin a half-hour start
and still beat him across the ocean
i mean i'm so bad i gave a falcon
a half-mile lead and beat him to the top of the
    mountain
i roared so loud the lion hung his head
in shame and his wife came and asked me to
    please
leave that part of the jungle as her husband's
    feelings
were so hurt by my together thing
i had a jumping contest with a kangaroo and
jumped clear outa australia and passed the
    astronauts
on their way back down
i can rap so hard Rap Brown hates to be
in the same town with me
and i'm only ten
this year coming

Nikki Giovanni

For Nkemdilim, my daughter

Nkemdilim, Nkemdilim,
run to me!
Do not stand there
making your cheeks swell out
like two big red tomatoes.
Do not push out your lips
like two red cherries
making figure eight.
Do not turn in your toes
like a duck,
making letter O

Nkemdilim – oo!
run to me, I say,
before I make your bottom red too
like the ripe tomatoes
of your sulky face!

Ifi Amadiume

Rope Rhyme

Get set, ready now, jump right in
Bounce and kick and giggle and spin
Listen to the rope when it hits the ground
Listen to that clappedy-slappedy sound
Jump right up when it tells you to
Come back down whatever you do
Count to a hundred, count by ten
Start to count all over again
That's what jumping is all about
Get set, ready now,
                         jump
                              right
                                   out!

Eloise Greenfield

Skipping Rope Song

Salt, vinegar, mustard, pepper,
If I dare,
I can do better,
who says no?
cause hens don't crow!
Salt, vinegar, mustard, pepper.

Salt, vinegar, mustard, pepper,
I wanna be great,
a hot shot lawyer,
a famous dancer,
a tough operator,
Salt, vinegar, mustard, pepper.

Salt, vinegar, mustard, pepper,
If I dare,
I can do better,
who cares from zero,
that hens don't crow,
Salt, vinegar, mustard, pepper.

Dionne Brand

Bed Time

Can i stay up five
minutes more let me
finish this book
Can't I finish this
bead chain
Can't I finish this
castle
       Can't I
       stay up
five minutes or four
three minutes or two
minutes one minute more.

Accabre Huntley

Tables

Headmaster a come, mek has'e! Si-down,
Amy! min' yuh bruck Jane collar-bone,
Tom! Tek yuh foot off o' de desk,
Sandra Wallace, mi know yuh vex
But beg yuh get off o' Joseph head.
Tek de lizard off o' Sue neck, Ted!
Sue, mi dear, don bawl so loud,
Thomas, yuh can tell mi why yuh a put de toad
Eena Elvira sandwich bag?
An, Jim, whey yuh a do wid dah bull frog?
Tek i' off mi table! yuh mad?
Mi know yuh chair small, May, but it not dat bad
Dat yuh haffe siddung pon de floor!
Jim don' squeeze de frog unda de door,
Put i' through de window – no, no Les!
Mi know yuh hungry, but Mary yeas
Won' full yuh up, so spit it out.
Now go wash de blood outa yuh mout.
Hortense, tek Mary to de nurse.
Nick tek yuh han out o' Mary purse!
Ah wonda who tell all o' yuh
Sey dat dis class-room is a zoo?
Si-down, Head-master comin' through de door!
"Two ones are two, two twos are four."

Valerie Bloom

Lazybones

Lazybones, let's go to the farm
    Sorry, I've got a headache
Lazybones, let's go pounding grain
    Sorry, my leg isn't right
Lazybones, let's go fetch firewood
    Sorry, my hands are hurting
Lazybones, come and have some food
    Hold on, let me wash my hands!

Malawi

43

A Man With a Hat On

A man with a hat on, I say no:
How should I know he is bald,
Bald, bald, nothing but bald,
Yes, indeed, nothing but bald?

A man with trousers on, I say no:
How should I know he is bow-legged,
Bow-legged, bow-legged, nothing but
   bow-legged,
Yes, indeed, nothing but bow-legged?

A man with glasses on, I say no:
How should I know he has a squint,
A squint, a squint, nothing but a squint,
Yes, indeed, nothing but a squint?

A man with shoes on, I say no:
How should I know his toes have jiggers,
Jiggers, jiggers, nothing but jiggers,
Yes, indeed, nothing but jiggers?

Malawi

Telephone

I am a telephone
I have heard
Many voices in confidence
I ring and they jump,
And pick up
My hand set.
Then they get set
For a talk.
'Hullo, who's speaking?'
'It's me' and they continue
In topics legal and illegal
They indulge in conversation
They think is all secret
But I listen
And wait like a computer
For the day I will be summoned
As witness
To all the dialogues
That transpired
That will be, the day of judgement.

Mamman J. Vatsa

Kid Stuff

The wise guys
tell me
that Christmas
is Kid Stuff . . .
Maybe they've got
something there—
Two thousand years ago
three wise guys
chased a star
across a continent
to bring
frankincense and myrrh
to a Kid
born in a manger
with an idea in his head . . .

And as the bombs
crash
all over the world today
the real wise guys know
that we've all got to go
chasing stars
again
in the hope
that we can get back
some of that
Kid Stuff
born two thousand years ago.

Frank Horne

Xmas

I forgot to send
A card to Jennie—
But the truth about cousins is
There's too many.

I also forgot
My Uncle Joe
But I believe I'll let
That old rascal go.

I done bought
Four boxes now
I can't afford
No more, no how.

So Merrry Xmas,
Everybody!
Cards or no cards
Here's HOWDY!

Langston Hughes

POOR FOWL and OTHER CREATURES

Poor Fowl

Fowl, condolences, poor, poor, poor fowl;
Fowl, condolences, poor, poor, poor fowl;
When a child is sick
I am looking for a fowl to buy:
When an old man is sick
I am looking for a fowl to buy:
When my wife is sick
I am looking for a fowl to buy:
When my brother is sick
I am looking for a fowl to buy:
Fowl, condolences, poor, poor, poor fowl!

Ghana

The Cat-Eyed Owl

The cat-eyed owl, although so fierce
At night with kittens and with mice

In daylight may be mobbed
By flocks of little birds, and in
The market-place, be robbed

Of all his dignity and wisdom
By children market-women and malingering men

Who hoot at it and mocking its myopic
Eyes, shout: 'Look!
Look at it now, he hangs his head in
Shame.' This never happens to the eagle
Or the nightingale.

Edward Kamau Brathwaite

Feeding the Pastor

She caught a chicken and wrung its neck.
She had already cooked a roast,
But she wanted to load the table
So he could eat and boast.

The pastor came right on time
And headed for the table,
He tucked a napkin under his chin
And ate what he was able.

He drove away in a cadillac
Like so many black preachers do,
Since she was good at wringing necks
She should have wrung his too.

Elma Stuckley

Charley and Miss Morley's Goat

Charley's mother went to town
Run, Charley, run
With a red hat on and a purple gown.
Run, Charley, run

Before she left she told the boys
Run, Charley, run
"You all stay home and play with your toys."
Run, Charley, run

Charley's brother and sister too
Run, Charley, run
Cleaned up the yard. What did he do?
Run, Charley, run

He dashed with friends up and down the street.
Run, Charley, run
Then Miss Morley's goat they began to beat
Run, Charley, run

The goat cried, 'Ma-a-a!' Miss Morley woke.
Run, Charley, run
When she saw the boys she was vexed and spoke:
Run, Charley, run

'Why don't you leave my goat alone?
Run, Charley, run
Charles, I'll tell your mother when she
    comes home.'
Run, Charley, run

Bad as her word, when the jitney brought Mom,
Run, Charley, run
Miss Morley told her about her son.
Run, Charley, run

Under the bed, Charley heard Mom say,
Run, Charley, run
'I'm going to fix his skin today!'
Run, Charley, run

'Come out here, Charles, and I mean
    RIGHT NOW.'
Run, Charley, run
'Who told you to leave this yard, anyhow?'
Run, Charley, run

Charley was spanked and sent to bed
Run, Charley, run
For not doing what his mama said.
Run, Charley, run

Telcine Turner

Herman Louis Montefiore

Herman Louis Montefiore
guards my great
grandmother's door.
He sits there, motionless
all day.
He never goes outside to play
He never sleeps, he never barks
He never romps or goes for larks.
He's the oddest strangest dog
as fluffy as a golliwog.
He's charcoal black and ashes grey
His eyes are bright but never gay.
I never ever met a pet
as Herman Louis Montefiore
who guards my great
grandmother's door.

Pamela Mordecai

The Clash

Such a quarrel and tangle.
Such terrible yapping bites.
Yelps frantic and claws frantic.
Snarling noise of both
a total terror.
No dog could let the other go.
They split only when punctured enough –
one off home limping,
the other with a woeful whimpering.

James Berry

Don't Call Alligator Long-Mouth Till You Cross River

Call alligator long-mouth
call alligator saw-mouth
call alligator pushy-mouth
call alligator scissors-mouth
call alligator raggedy-mouth
call alligator bumpy-bum
call alligator all dem rude word
but better wait
                till you cross river.

John Agard

59

Sensemaya

Chant for killing a snake

Mayombe-bombe-mayombe!
Mayombe-bombe-mayombe!
Mayombe-bombe-mayombe!

The serpent has eyes made of glass;
the serpent comes, wraps itself round a stick;
with its eyes made of glass, round a stick,
with its eyes made of glass.
The serpent walks without any legs;
the serpent hides in the grass;
walking hides in the grass,
walking without any legs.

Mayombe-bombe-mayombe!
Mayombe-bombe-mayombe!
Mayombe-bombe-mayombe

Hit it with the axe, and it dies;
hit it now!
Don't hit it with your foot, it will bite you,
Don't hit it with your foot, it will flee!

Sensemaya, the serpent,
sensemaya.
Sensemaya, with his eyes,
sensemaya.
Sensemaya, with his tongue,
sensemaya.
Sensemaya, with his mouth,
sensemaya.

The dead serpent cannot eat,
the dead serpent cannot hiss;
cannot walk,
cannot run.
The dead serpent cannot see;
the dead serpent cannot drink;
cannot breathe,
cannot bite!

Mayombe-bombe-mayombe!
Sesemaya, the serpent . . .
Mayombe-bombe-mayombe!
Sensemaya, is not moving . . .
Mayombe-bombe-mayombe!
Sensemaya, the serpent . . .
Mayombe-bombe-mayombe!
Sensemaya, he is dead!

Nicalás Guillén

The Tangled Cow

The tame white cow trapped
In the tangle of a mangrove
Moans against the roar of waves
And butts wildly at stumps and trees.

Spotted white
With swollen eyelids,
Breasts dripping milk into the dark water,
She foams at the mouth.

At evening the owner scours
The field on familiar tracks, but
His young son hears the soft moaning
And rushes in, leaping over the bent growth.

She licks his hand,
And he walks with her
Into the open pasture
Like a man beside his mother.

Jagdip Maraj

HARD TIMES/WORK TIMES

Poem

Click, clack, click, clack
That's all I hear every day
I am so tired of all this
Typing
I must get away
I must get away
Is this all to life
Nothing more
Nothing real
What a bore
Click, clack, click, clack
Looking up
Through the dirty panes
I see a sunset so beautiful
It takes my breath away
I am lost in reverie
Smiling, my tired eyes
Seem refreshed and
Suddenly life takes on
A new look
Click, clack, click, clack

Anne Wallace

An Elder's Prayer

O Great Spirit of my fores
I have nothing in my hand
But a chicken and some rice
To make sacrifice to you,
This is all my land can give,
Bring us sunshine with the rains
So the harvest wind can blow,
Save my people from all pains
When the harvest time is done
I will make a feast to you.

African Oral Tradition

Busted

My bills are all due and the baby needs shoes, and
   I'm busted
Cotton is down to a quarter a pound, but
   I'm busted
I got a cow that went dry and a hen that won't lay
And a big stack of bills that gets bigger each day
The county's gonna haul my belongings, 'cause
   I'm busted

I went to my brother and ask for a loan, 'cause
    I'm busted
I hate to beg like a dog without his bone, but
    I'm busted
My brother said, 'There ain't a thing I can do
My wife and kids are all down with the flu
And I was just thinking of calling on you, and
    I'm busted.'

Well I am no thief but a man can go wrong, when
    he's busted
The food that we canned all last summer is gone,
    and I'm busted
The fields are all bare and the cotton won't grow
Me and my family got to pack up and go
But I'll make a living, just where I don't know
'Cause I'm busted
I'm broke . . . no bread . . . I mean like nothin'
    . . . forget it . . .

Harlan Howard

Hunger

This is hunger. An animal
all fangs and eyes.
It cannot be distracted or deceived.
It is not satisfied with one meal.
It is not content
with a lunch or a dinner.
Always threatens blood.
Roars like a lion, squeezes like a boa,
thinks like a person.

The specimen before you
was captured in India (outskirts of Bombay)
but it exists in a more or less savage state
in many other places.

Please stand back.

Nicalás Guillén

My Telly

My telly eats people
especially on the news

Little people   My telly
with no shoes   eats people
Little people   If you don't
with no food   believe me
Little people   look inside
crying   the belly
Little people   of my telly
dying

John Agard

My country

(For Mandela)

I stand by the gate
School's out
Smoke fills the location
Tears come to my eyes

I wipe them away
I walk into the kitchen
To see my mother's
Black hard-working hands
A forceful smile from
A tired face

We sit and have supper
I pick up a picture of
My father and look
My mother turns away
Tries to hide

My father left my mother
In his arms
He is roughly separated
From her

The van pulls away
Mother watches bravely enough
I as a child do
Not understand

My heart aches
How I long to see my father
At least to hold his hand
And comfort him
Or at least to tell him
He'll be back some day.

Zinziswa Mandela (at the age of twelve)

Prayer for Rain

Chauta we beseech you, we beseech you!
You have refused us rain, we beseech you!
The whole land has dried up, we beseech you!
Give us rain today, we beseech you!
We are concerned, we beseech you!
Have mercy on us, we beseech you!
Do not abandon us your children, we
    beseech you!
Do not harden your heart against us, we
    beseech you!
Send us rain, we beseech you!

Malawi

Life

Life is playing me up
Spite is having an affair with me
It thinks it hurts me
But it don't
Life is hard
I wish I didn't come here at all.

Once I was able to go into the record room
Not any more
It has been stopped
Why, I don't know.
But I have an idea
The one which could be true.

It is no longer my heart
That is broken
But my brain
It is confused.

Vivian Usherwood

Looking At Your Hands

No!
I will not still my voice!
I have
too much to claim –
if you see me
looking at books
or coming to your house
or walking in the sun
know that I look for fire!

I have learnt
from books dear friend
of men dreaming and living
and hungering in a room without a light
who could not die since death was far too poor
who did not sleep to dream, but dreamed to
   change the world!

And so
if you see me
looking at your hands
listening when you speak
marching in your ranks
you must know
I do not sleep to dream, but dream to change
   the world!

Martin Carter

Market Women

Down from the hills, they come
With swinging hips and steady stride
To feed the hungry Town
They stirred the steep dark land
To place within the growing seed.
And in the rain and sunshine
Tended the young green plants,
They bred, and dug and reaped.
And now, as Heaven has blessed their toil,
They come, bearing the fruits,
These hand-maids of the Soil,
Who bring full baskets down,
To feed the hungry Town.

Daisy Myrie

Song of the Banana Man

Tourist, white man wiping his face,
Met me in Golden Grove market place.
He looked at my old clothes brown with stain
And soaked right through with the Portland rain.
He cast his eye, and turned up his nose
And said, 'You're a beggar man I suppose,'
He said, 'Boy get some occupation,
Be of some value to your nation.'

I said, 'By God and this big right hand
You must recognise a banana man.'

Up in the hills where the streams are cool,
Where mullet and janga swim in the pool,
I have ten acres of mountain side
And a dainty foot donkey that I ride
Four Gros Michel and four Lacatan
Some coconut trees and some hills of yam
And I pasture on that very same land
Five she goats and a big black ram.

That, by God and this big right hand
Is the property of the banana man.

I leave my yard early morning time
And set my foot to the mountain climb
I bend my back for the hot-sun toil
And my cutlass rings on the stony soil,
Clearing and weeding, digging and planting,
Till Massa sun drop back a John Crow mountain
Then home again in cool evening time
Perhaps whistling this little rhyme,

Praise God and this big right hand
I will live and die a banana man.

Banana day is my special day
I cut my stems and I'm on the way
Load up the donkey, leave the land
Head down the hill to banana stand,
When the truck comes down I take a ride
All the way down to the harbour side;
That is the night when you tourist man
Would change your place with a banana man.

Yes, praise God and my big right hand
I will live and die a banana man.

The bay is calm and the moon is bright
The hills look black though the sky is light
Down at the dock is an English ship
Resting after her ocean trip
While on the pier is a monstrous hustle
Tally men, carriers all in a bustle
With the stems on their heads in a long black
    snake
Some singing the songs that banana men make.

Like Praise God and my big right hand
I will live and die a banana man.

Then the payment comes and we have some fun
Me, Zekiel, Breda and Duppy Son
Down at the bar near United wharf,
Knock back a white rum, bus' a laugh
Fill the empty bag for further toil
With saltfish, breadfruit and coconut oil
Then head back home to my yard to sleep
A proper sleep that is long and deep.

Yes, praise God and my big right hand
I will live and die a banana man.

So when you see these old clothes brown with
    stain
And soaked clean through with Portland rain
Don't cast your eyes nor turn your nose
Don't judge a man by his patchy clothes
I'm a strong man a proud man and I'm free
Part of these mountains part of this sea
I know myself and I know my ways
And will say with pride to the end of my days,

Praise God and my big right hand
I will live and die a banana man.

Evan Jones

Boy on a Swing

Slowly he moves
to and fro, to and fro,
then faster and faster
he swishes up and down.

His blue shirt
billows in the breeze
like a tattered kite.

The world whirls by:
east becomes west,
north turns to south;
the four cardinal points
meet in his head.

      Mother!
Where did I come from?
When will I wear long trousers?
Why was my father jailed?

Mbuyiseni Oswald Mtshali

WAY DOWN IN THE MUSIC

Way Down in the Music

I get way down in the music
Down inside the music
I let it wake me
          take me
Spin me around and make me
Uh-get down

Inside the sound of the Jackson Five
Into the tune of Earth, Wind and Fire
Down in the bass where the beat comes from
Down in the horn and down in the drum
I get down
I get down

I get way down in the music
Down inside the music
I let it wake me
       take me

Spin me around and shake me
I get down down
I get down

Eloise Greenfield

Boxer Man In-A Skippin Workout

Skip on big man, steady steady.
Giant, skip-dance easy easy!
Broad and tall a-work shaped limbs,
a-move sleek self with style well trimmed.
Gi rhythm your ease in bein strong.
Movement is a meanin and a song.
    Tek your little trips in your skips, man.
    Be that dancer-runner man.

You so easy easy. Go-on na big man!
Fighter man is a rhythm man
full of go fine and free.
Movement is a dream and a spree.
You slow down, you go fast.
Sweat come oil your body like race horse.
    Tek your little trips in your skips, man.
    Be that dancer-runner man – big man!

James Berry

Poetry Jump-Up

Tell me if ah seeing right
Take a look down de street

Words dancin
words dancin
till dey sweat
words like fishes
jumpin out a net
words wild and free
joinin de poetry revelry
words back to back
words belly to belly

Come on everybody
come and join de poetry band
dis is poetry carnival
dis is poetry bacchanal
when inspiration call
take yu pen in yu hand
if yu dont have a pen
take yu pencil in yu hand
if you dont have a pencil
what the hell
so long de feeling start to swell
just shout de poem out

Words jumpin off de page
tell me if Ah seeing right
words like birds
jumpin out a cage
take a look down de street
words shakin dey waist
words shakin dey bum
words wit black skin
words wit white skin
words wit brown skin
words wit no skin at all
words huggin up words
an saying I want to be a poem today
rhyme or no rhyme
I is a poem today
I mean to have a good time

Words feelin hot hot hot
big words feelin hot hot hot
lil words feelin hot hot hot
even sad words cant help
tappin dey toe
to de riddum of de poetry band

Dis is poetry carnival
dis is poetry bacchanal
so come on everybody
join de celebration
all yu need is plenty perspiration
an a little inspiration
plenty perspiration
an a little inspiration

John Agard

Beat Drummers

Come Zipporah come rock with I
songs of praise to set spirit high,
drummers beat drummers beat,
we were never here to stay
hear that sound from far away,
drummers beat, drummers beat,
beat drummers beat 'cause the beat well sweet
beat down the beat that cools the heat,
drummers beat, drummers beat.

Come little children rock with I
the beat of the drum will never die,
drummers beat, drummers beat,
drum beat sound will never drown
listen to the beat as the beat beats a hard,
drummers beat, drummers beat,
beat drummers beat and beat it hard
beat it like you beat and when you beat it
    back a yard,
drummers beat, drummers beat,
beat drummers, beat drummers beat
    drummers beat.

Benjamin Zephaniah

Song for a Banjo Dance

Shake your brown feet, honey,
Shake your brown feet, chile,
Shake your brown feet, honey,
Shake 'em swift and wil'—
   Get way back, honey,
   Do that rockin' step.
   Slide on over, darling,
     Now! Come out
     With your left.
Shake your brown feet, honey,
Shake 'em, honey chile.

Sun's going down this evening—
Might never rise no mo'.
The sun's going down this very night—
Might never rise no mo'
So dance with swift feet, honey,
   (The banjo's sobbing low)
Dance with swift feet, honey—
   Might never dance no mo'.

Shake your brown feet, Liza,
Shake 'em, Liza, chile,
Shake your brown feet, Liza,
   (The music's soft and wil')
Shake your brown feet, Liza,
   (The banjo's sobbing low)
The sun's going down this very night—
Might never rise no mo'.

Langston Hughes

Dancing Poinciana

Fire in the treetops,
Fire in the sky.
Blossoms red as sunset
Dazzling to the eye.

Dance, Poinciana,
Sway, Poinciana,
On a sea of green.
Dance, Poinciana,
Regal as a queen.

Fire in the treetops,
Fire in the sky.
Crimson petals and white
Stained with scarlet dye.

Dance, Poinciana,
Sway, Poinciana,
On a sea of green.
Dance Poinciana,
Sway, Poinciana,
Regal as a queen.

Telcine Turner

MAGIC AND OLD DAYS

Old Men of Magic

Old men of magic
with beards long and aged,
speak tales on evenings,
tales so entrancing,
we sit and we listen,
to whispery secrets
about the earth and the heavens.
And late at night,
after sundown they speak
of spirits that live
in silk cotton trees,
of frightening shadows
that sneak through the dark,
and bright balls of fire
that fly in night air,
of shapes unimaginable,
we gasp and we gape,
then just as we're scared
old men of magic
wave hands rough and wrinkled
and all trace of fear disappears.

Dionne Brand

For Ma

Roll roti! roll roti! roll roti! roll roti!
Curry cooking in de karahee
Bora boilin wid de bagee
Woodsmoke sweet in me nose like agarbattee—
Ayuh wake up wake up ayuh pickni wake up
ayuh man
Wid de sunshine in yu eye an de river a flow
An brung doves burstin from de trees an de
kiskidees
And de whole savannah swimmin green an a
glow!

Wata foh fetch battam-house foh daub fresh
bucket foh mend clothes foh beat
Wake up ayuh pickni wuk no dun wuk foh duh
Cutlass foh shaap wood foh chap fence foh build
dat bull bruk dung
Is wha da maan stretch e haan an yaan foh!
Hear a cow baal in de yaad how dem swell wid
milk-fraff
Goat a groan dem want go graze an sheep a
caff-caff—
Ayu wake up wake up time no deh foh cry time
na deh foh laff
Hen a lay an cow a drap time na deh foh stap!

David Dabydeen

Duppy Dan

Duppy Dan
aint no livin man

Duppy Dan
done dead an gone

Duppy Dan
nah have foot

Duppy Dan
nah have hand

Yet Duppy Dan cross water
Duppy Dan cross land

Duppy Dan ride white horse
pon pitchdark night

Run like-a-hell stranger
when Duppy Dan tell you goodnight

John Agard

Full Moon

Full moon is the nicest time
For telling 'Nancy story
Except the ones 'bout snake and ghost
Because they are so scary

Hide and seek is nice then too
Because it's light as day
And mamas don't say it's too late
If you go out to play

Odette Thomas

I Like to Stay Up

I like to stay up
and listen
when big people talking
jumbie stories

I does feel
so tingly and excited
inside me

But when my mother say
'Girl, time for bed'

Then is when
I does feel a dread

Then is when
I does cover up
from me feet to me head

Then is when
I does wish I didn't listen
to no stupid jumbie story

Then is when
I does wish I did read
me book instead

Grace Nichols

Jumbie — Guyanese word for ghost

Electric Eel Song

Ay! me one child Ay-eeee!
Ay! me one daughter
Take out you' foot
From the black river water
Haul out you' hand
Out the slow river water
Stay 'pon the bank
Of the cold river water
Ay! me one daughter
Ay! me one child! Ay-eeee!

Electric eel
Is the eel in the river
Shadow 'pon the bottom
Is the eel in the river
Something like you' hand
Is the eel in the river
Swimming like you' foot
Is the eel in the river

Ay! me one child! Ay-eeee!
Ay! me one daughter
Foot after foot
Through the black river water
She can't touch the bottom
Of the slow river water
Shirt like umbrella
In the cold riverwater
Ay! me one daughter
Ay! me one child! Ay-eeee!

Electric eel
Is the eel in the river
Cutlass shape
Is the eel in the river
Black blade or brown
Is the eel in the river
Dozing so quiet
Is the eel in the river

Ay! me one child! Ay-eeee!
Ay! me one daughter!
Slap of a tail
Through the black river water
Shiver like ague
In the slow river water
As if she take cramp
From the cold river water
Ay! me one daughter!
Ay! me one child! Ay-eeee!

Electric eel
Is the eel in the river
No blood, just a thrill
Is the eel in the river
Lightning bold
Is the eel in the river
And she drown now, she chilly
Is the eel in the river

Ay! me one daughter
Ay! me one child! Ay-eeee!

Slade Hopkinson

They

they tapped and tapped on the shell
and the shell broke
and the yolk broke

cracked they said it's cracked

then they opened the cracked shell wide
  and cried

                        and cried

Mervyn Morris

Anancy

Anancy is a spider;
Anancy is a man;
Anancy's West Indian
And West African.

Sometimes, he wears a waistcoat;
Sometimes, he carries a cane;
Sometimes, he sports a top hat;
Sometimes, he's just a plain,
Ordinary, black, hairy spider.

Anancy is vastly cunning,
Tremendously greedy,
Excessively charming,
Hopelessly dishonest,
Warmly loving,
Firmly confident,
Fiercely wild,
A fabulous character,
Completely out of our mind
And out of his, too.

Anancy is a master planner,
A great user
Of other people's plans;
He pockets everybody's food,
Shelter, land, money, and more;
He achieves mountains of things,
Like stolen flour dumplings;
He deceives millions of people,
Even the man in the moon;
And he solves all the mysteries
On earth, in air, under sea.

And always,
Anancy changes
From a spider into a man
And from a man into a spider
And back again
At the drop of a sleepy eyelid.

Andrew Salkey

Mama Dot

Born on a sunday
in the kingdom of Ashante

Sold on monday
into slavery

Ran away on tuesday
cause she born free

Lost a foot on wednesday
when they catch she

Worked all thursday
till her head grey

Dropped on friday
where they burned she

Freed on saturday
in a new century

Fred D'Aguiar

Harriet Tubman

Freedom Fighter
About 1823-1913
Maryland, USA.

'Miss Moses' people called her,
For she was very brave.
She opened the doors of freedom
To help the hopeful slave.

She led her folk from bondage
On many, many trips;
A gun beneath her cloak but
A prayer on her lips!

Sometimes they grew so frightened
Their bodies quaked with fears.
She nudged them with her gun and
Then wiped away their tears!

She slipped behind the Rebel lines;
A Union spy was she,
She burned their crops and freed their slaves,
Then left to set more free!

Eloise Crosby Culver

Lineage

My grandmothers were strong.
They followed plows and bent to toil.
They moved through fields sowing seed.
They touched earth and grain grew.
They were full of sturdiness and singing.
My grandmothers were strong.

My grandmothers are full of memories
Smelling of soap and onions and wet clay
With veins rolling roughly over quick hands
They have many clean words to say.
My grandmothers were strong.
Why am I not as they?

Margaret Walker

sugarfields

treetalk and windsong
are the language of my mother
her music does not leave me.

let me taste again the cane
the syrup of the earth
sugarfields were once my home.

I would lie down in the fields
and never get up again
(treetalk and windsong
are the language of my mother
sugarfields are my home)

the leaves go on whispering secrets
as the wind blows a tune in the grass
my mother's voice is in the fields
this music cannot leave me.

Barbara Mahone

Tell Me Trees
What Are You Whispering?

It is strange
Standing here
Beneath the whispering trees
Far away from the haunts of men.
Tell me trees!
What are you whispering?

When I am dead
I shall come and lie
Beneath your fallen leaves . . .
But tell me trees.
What are you whispering?

They shall bury me
Beneath your fallen leaves.
My robe shall be
Green, fallen leaves.
My love shall be
Fresh, fallen leaves.
My lips shall kiss
Sweet, fallen leaves.
I and the leaves shall lie together
Never parting . . .
I and the leaves shall always lie together
And know no parting.

It is so strange
Standing here
Beneath the whispering trees!
Tell me, trees!
What are you whispering?

Wilson Harris

On Aging

When you see me sitting quietly,
Like a sack left on the shelf,
Don't think I need your chattering.
I'm listening to myself.
Hold! Stop! Don't pity me!
Hold! Stop your sympathy!
Understanding if you got it,
Otherwise I'll do without it!

When my bones are stiff and aching
And my feet won't climb the stair,
I will only ask one favour:
Don't bring me no rocking chair.

When you see me walking, stumbling,
Don't study and get it wrong.
'Cause tired don't mean lazy
And every goodbye ain't gone.
I'm the same person I was back then,
A little less hair, a little less chin,
A lot less lungs and much less wind.
But ain't I lucky I can still breathe in.

Maya Angelou

A TASTE OF ASIA

The Rich Eat Three Full Meals

The rich eat three full meals, the poor two small
bowls,
But peace is what matters.
Thirsty, I drink sweet plum tea;
Warm, I lie in the shade, in the breeze;
My paintings are mountains and rivers all around
me,
My damask, embroidered, the grass.
I rest at night, rest easy,
Am awake with the sun
And enjoying Heaven's heaped-up favors.

Nguyen Binh Khiem

Feeding the Poor at Christmas

Every Christmas we feed the poor.
We arrive an hour late: Poor dears,
Like children waiting for a treat.
Bring your plates. Don't move.
Don't try turning up for more.
No. Even if you don't drink
you can't take your share
for your husband. Say thank you
and a rosary for us every evening.

No. Not a towel and a shirt,
even if they're old.
What's that you said?
You're a good man, Robert, yes,
beggars can't be, exactly.

Eunice de Souza

Chaitanya

come off it
said chaitanya to a stone
in stone language

wipe the red paint off your face
i don't think the colour suits you
i mean what's wrong
with being just a plain stone
i'll still bring you flowers
you like the flowers of zendu
don't you
i like them too

Jejuri Arun Kolatkar

The Butterfly

There is no story behind it.
It is split like a second.
It hinges around itself.

It has no future.
It is pinned down to no past.
It's a pun on the present.

It's a little yellow butterfly.
It has taken these wretched hills
under its wings.

Just a pinch of yellow,
it opens before it closes
and closes before it o

where is it

Jejuri Arun Kolatkar

An Umbrella and a Watch

Father gave me,
while I was still a child, a little
umbrella and a watch.

He was six feet tall
and his umbrella would be
two or three feet above him.
So when I, a three-foot
dwarf,
walked by his side in rain,
my body would all be wet and muddy.
              While going
my left side would be wet, while coming
my right side.
              His creaking chappals
would raise at every step a spray of mud
from top to toe.
              Even after the rain stopped
It would fall drip drop drip
on my head.
'Ah, poor chap!' father would say,
bend and walk like a dwarf
and lower his umbrella:
that would make me laugh and laugh indeed.

But
when he lowered his umbrella
my eyes, nose and neck would be in
danger: the umbrella wires would peck me
with their ends.
It is very difficult to walk
under father's umbrella.
So he got me an umbrella
and with it, as a keepsake, a new watch.

After I had the new umbrella,
father would hold his under the rain
and I mine
under his.

But
brother played donkey with my umbrella
and broke its stick. One Sunday a storm
turned the black cloth
upside down.
                    As for the watch,
it worked for a week and then stopped.
I was angry
and put it in granny's betel-nut grinder
and pounded it away.

Mother
gave me a piece of her mind and beat me
and cleared it by sweeping away
its wheels, spring, hands and feet.

For many days
poor granny, toothless except for two teeth,
would pound betel-leaves, arecanuts and all
and while chewing would say:
'Why, Ramu, it tastes as though
a wheel or a tooth of a watch
has been ground into it.'

A.K. Ramanujan

(Translated by S.K. Desai)

If One Wants that Bird

You know,
there was a king in Mongolia,
                who once invaded some
distant kingdom, where
he heard a new bird singing,
and wanted the song for himself.
For the sake of the song, he wished to capture
the bird, with the bird its nest,
the branches that held the nest,
the trunk of the tree, the tree itself,
the roots, the earth that held the roots,
the village,
the water,
the surrounding land,
the country,
the entire kingdom . . .
                Wanting to take them all
he gathered together all the remaining
elephants, horses, chariots
and soldiers,
conquered the entire kingdom,
annexed it to his empire

and never returned home.

A.K. Ramanujan

(Translated by S.K. Desai)

Reasons For Extinction

Dodos do
nothing to
dastards who
do dodos down.

Dog-god does
not defend
dodos being
undone.

Dodos lovey-dovey
with dodo darlings
don't become
dodo dams or dads.

Dodos do
dumb things
like Dido or
dinosaurs did.

Do dodos die
out.

H.O. Nazareth

Conversations

Sitting in class,
listening to
conversations.
Eddy and Frog
playing cards,
'I never put that down.'
'Yes you did.'

'Shame,' says Alrick.

Kevin P. casually
beating up
Kevin B.
'Get off,'
'Shut your gob.'

Butts and Byron
doing their work,
for once,
'What about number seven?'
'Me no know.'

Tina and the two Lesleys,
talking,
'She went out last night.'
'You never believe who I saw yesterday.'

Nisha, Nayyar and Sumathi
listen to
Jackie and Claudia
arguing,
'Stop writing on my book!'
'Bloody well leave off!'

Errol points out
the window,
Dapo answers him,
'Fisk.'
'Shame.'

Tracey, Janet and Gaby
talk amongst themselves,
loudly,
'Have you done your homework?'
'Staying dinners?'

Sir stands up
'4i please be quiet!'
Mr Munro is now in
tears.

Marie and Pauline
writing,
on the desk,
'Did you see that film last night?'
'We've got French.'

Ashok and Ramji,
quiet.

Gary, Dean and Lee,
fighting,
'Stop strangling me!'
'You git.'

'I wonder why sir's got his head on the desk?'

Deepak Kalha

A Conjugation

Pretence, to pretend, I pretend,
You pretend, we pretend,
They pretend.

I pretend, you pretended,
We pretended, they pretended.

I will pretend, you will pretend,
We will pretend, they will pretend.

Pretence, to pretend, I will not pretend,
You will not pretend, we will not pretend,
They will not pretend.

No more pretence. An end
To pretension.

Nissim Ezekiel

Night of the Scorpion

I remember the night my mother
was stung by a scorpion. Ten hours
of steady rain had driven him
to crawl beneath a sack of rice.
Parting with his poison – flash
of diabolic tail in the dark room–
he risked the rain again.
The peasants came like swarms of flies
and buzzed the Name of God a hundred times
to paralyse the Evil One.
With candles and with lanterns
throwing giant scorpion shadows
on the mud-baked walls
they searched for him: he was not found.
They clicked their tongues.
With every movement that the scorpion made
his poison moved in Mother's blood, they said.
May he sit still, they said.
May the sins of your previous birth
be burned away tonight, they said.
May your suffering decrease
the misfortunes of your next birth, they said.
May the sun of evil
balanced in this unreal world
against the sun of good
become diminished by your pain.

May the poison purify your flesh
of desire, and your spirit of ambition,
they said, and they sat around
on the floor with my mother in the centre,
the peace of understanding on each face.
More candles, more lanterns, more neighbours,
more insects, and the endless rain.
My mother twisted through and through
groaning on a mat.
My father, sceptic, rationalist,
trying every curse and blessing,
powder, mixture, herb and hybrid.
He even poured a little paraffin
upon the bitten toe and put a match to it.
I watched the flame feeding on my mother.
I watched the holy man perform his rites
to tame the poison with an incantation.
After twenty hours
it lost its sting.

My mother only said,
Thank God the scorpion picked on me
and spared my children.

Nissim Ezekiel

Maths

What do you minus,
and from where?
I ask my teacher,
but he don't care.

Ten cubic metres
in square roots,
Or how many toes
go in nine boots?

Change ten decimals
to a fraction
Aaaaaaaaaaahhhhhhhhhh!
is my reaction.

Deepak Kalha

Moment

Among the dustbins
and scrawny cats
yellowing newspapers
and broken slats
a moment of beauty
breaks in the gutter
as rainclouds part
and the moon peeps
and is caught
in a rainbow puddle
of oil-slicked water.

Cecil Rajendra

Crab

Before you wipe your feet of dew,
Crab, Sir, a word with you.

The complex metre of your walk
Is a language poets talk.

Look, Sir, how crabby feet
Spin abstract magic on the street.

The eagle – whoosh! a giddy grab
Of claws – goodbye, Mr Crab.

P. Lal

Domestic Creatures

i. Pigeon

Swaddled cosily, he
Settles by the window,
Burping softly:
Eyelids half-closed
Head sinking
In a fluffy
Embroidered pillow.

ii. Cockroach

Open the lid, he tumbles out
Like a family secret;
Scuttles back into darkness;
Reappears, feelers like
Miniature periscopes,
Questioning the air;
Leaves tell-tale traces:
Shed wings flaky
As onion skin, fresh
Specks scurrying
In old crevices.

Manohar Shetty

Paper Boats

Day by day I float my paper boats one by one
    down the running stream.
In big black letters I write my name on them and
    the name of the village where I live.
I hope that someone in some strange land will find
    them and know who I am.
I load my little boats with shiuli flowers from our
    garden, and hope that these blooms of the dawn
    will be carried safely to land in the night.
I launch my paper boats and look into the sky and
    see the little clouds setting their white bulging
    sails.
I know not what playmate of mine in the sky
    sends them down the air to race with my boats!
When night comes I bury my face in my arms
    and dream that my paper boats float on and on
    under the midnight stars.
The fairies of sleep are sailing in them, and the
    lading is their baskets full of dreams.

Rabindranath Tagore

Index of First Lines

A heart to hate you 9
A man with a hat on, I say no 44
Among the dustbins 133
Anancy is a spider 106
As a child I worked this land half-naked 110
Ay! me one child Ay-eeee! 102
Before you wipe your feet of dew 134
Born on a sunday 108
Call alligator long-mouth 59
Can i stay up five 40
Charley's mother went to town 54
Chauta we beseech you, we beseech you! 72
Click, clack, click, clack 64
Come off it 118
Come Zipporah come rock with I 91
Day by day I float my paper boats one by one 137
Dodos do 125
Down from the hills, they come 76
Duppy Dan 98
Every Christmas we feed the poor 117
Father gave me 120
Fire in the treetops 94
Fowl, condolences, poor, poor, poor fowl 50
Fruit in a bowl 26
Full moon is the nicest time 99
Get set, ready now, jump right in 38
He hit me on the face, Mummy 30
Headmaster a come, mek has'e! Si-down 42
Herman Louis Montefiore 56
I always like summer 15
I am a telephone 45
i can run faster than any gazelle 36
I forgot to send 48
I get way down in the music 84
I have often wondered 12
I know a man a very funny man 32
I like to stay up 100

I love me mudder and me mudder love me   17
I love my Granny Anna   33
I love the   24
I pulled a humming bird out of the sky one day   13
I remember the night my mother   130
I stand by the gate   70
i wake to a yellow fire   23
It is strange   112
Just because I loves you-   18
Lazybones, let's go to the farm   43
Life is playing me up   74
Mayombe-bombe-mayombe!   60
Me don't want no hair style   20
Mek me tell you wha me Mudder do   34
'Miss Moses' people called her   109
My bills are all due and the baby needs shoes, and   66
My grandmothers were strong   110
My telly eats people   69
Nkemdilim, Nkemdilim   37
No!   75
O Great Spirit of my fores   65
Old men of magic   96
Once the wind   14
Open the lid, he tumbles out   136
Pretence, to pretend, I pretend   129
Roll Roti! roll roti! roll roti! roll roti!   97
Salt, vinegar, mustard, pepper   39
Shake your brown feet, honey   92
She caught a chicken and wrung its neck   52
Sitting in class   126
Skip on big man, steady steady   86
Slowly he moves   82
Some folks can live while other die   28
Such a quarrel and tangle   57
Swaddled cosily, he   136
Tell me if ah seeing right   88
The cat-eyed owl, although so fierce   51
The rich eat three full meals, the poor two small   116
The street is in darkness   22
The tame white cow trapped   62
The wise guys   46
There is no story behind it   119

They tapped and tapped on the shell   105
This is hunger. An animal   68
Tourist, white man wiping his face   78
treetalk and windsong   111
Under the soursop silver-leaf tree   31
What do you minus   132
When you see me sitting quietly   114
You ever feel   19
You know   124

Acknowledgements

The author and the Publisher would like to thank the following for their kind permission to reprint copyright material in this book:

Precedent Publishing Inc. for 'Feeding the Pastor' and 'Ringmarole: Puzzles for children' by Elma Stuckley from *The Big Gate*; Oxford University Press for 'Night of the Scorpion' and 'A Conjugation' by Nissim Ezekiel, 'Boy on a Swing' by Mbuyiseni Oswald Mtshali from *Sounds of a Cowhide Drum* © 1971 Mbuyiseni Oswald Mtshali, 'An Umbrella and a Watch' and 'If One Wants That Bird' by A.K. Ramanujan; Onibonoje Press and Book Industries (Nig.) Ltd for 'Telephone' by Mamman J. Vatsa from *Verses for Children*; Eunice de Souza for 'Feeding the Poor at Christmas'; Edward Kamau Brathwaite for 'The Cat-Eyed Owl'; Bogle-L'Ouverture Publications Ltd for 'Moment' by Cecil Rajendra from *Hour of Assassins*, 'Full Moon' by Odette Thomas from *Rain Falling Sun Shining*, 'Bed Time' and 'Funny Man' by Accabre Huntley from *At School Today*; Dionne Brand for 'Wind', 'Skipping Rope Song' and 'Old Men of Magic'; Amon Saba Saakana for 'Watching the Sun'; Macmillan, London and Basingstoke for 'Paper Boats' by Rabindranath Tagore from *The Crescent Moon*, 'Charley and Miss Morley' and 'Dancing Poinciana' by Telcine Turner from *Song of the Surreys*; Manohar Shetty for 'Domestic Creatures: Pigeon; Cockroach'; Nikki Giovanni for 'Knoxville, Tennessee', © 1968 Nikki Giovanni; Nikki Giovanni and Collins Publishers, Toronto for 'a heavy rap'; The Viking Press, Inc, for 'Rope Rhyme' and 'Way Down in the Music' by Eloise Greenfield; Writers Workshop, Calcutta for 'Crab' by P. Lal from *The Collected Poems of P. Lal* © 1977 Writers Workshop, Calcutta; Centerprise Trust Ltd for 'Life' by Vivian Usherwood from *Poems*; Ian McDonald for 'Georgetown Children'; A.J. Seymour for 'Fruit in a Bowl'; Kamal Singh for 'Six O'Clock Feeling'; Dangaroo Press UK for 'For Ma' by David Dabydeen from *Slave Song*; The Bodley Head for 'Don't Call Alligator . . .' by John Agard from *Say it Again, Granny* and 'My Telly' by John Agard from *I Din Do Nuttin*; Oxford University Press and Andrew Salkey for 'Anancy'; Century Hutchinson Publishing

Group Limited for 'I Love Me Mudder' and 'Beat Drummers' by
Benjamin Zephaniah from *The Dread Affair*; Ifi Amadiume for
'For Nkemdilim, my daughter' from *Passion Waves*, Karnak
House 1985; The African National Congress of South Africa for
'My Country' by Zinziswa Mandela from *Malibongwe*; Evan
Jones for 'Song of the Banana Man'; Chatto and Windus for
'Mama Dot' by Fred D'Aguiar from *Mama Dot*; Wilson Harris
for 'Tell Me Trees What Are You Whispering'; Lesley Miranda
for 'Dread-lock Style' and 'Don't Hit Your Sister'; Yansan
Agard for 'To Granny Anna'; Grace Nichols for 'Wha Me
Mudder Do' and 'I Like to Stay Up'; John Agard for 'Poetry
Carnival' and 'Duppy Dan'; Broadside Press for 'The Beauty of
It' by Don L. Lee from *Black Pride*; Shake Keane for 'Once the
Wind'; 'Reasons Why' by Langston Hughes from *The Dream
Keeper and Other Poems* copyright © 1932 by Alfred A. Knopf,
Inc. and renewed 1960 by Langston Hughes, reprinted by
permission of Alfred A. Knopf, Inc. and David Higham
Associates; 'Song for a Banjo Dance' by Langston Hughes from
The Weary Blues, copyright © 1926 by Alfred A. Knopf Inc.
and renewed 1954 by Langston Hughes, reprinted by permission
of Alfred A. Knopf, Inc. and David Higham Associates; Martin
Carter for 'For My Son' and 'Looking at Your Hands'; Valerie
Bloom for 'Headmaster'; Simon & Schuster for 'Xmas' by
Langston Hughes and 'Kid Stuff' by Frank Horne; Pamela
Mordecai and Nelson Caribbean for 'Herman Louis Montefiore'
by Pamela Mordecai; James Berry for 'The Clash' and 'Boxer
Man In-a Skippin Workout'; Jagdip Maraj for 'The Tangled
Cow'; Nicalás Guillén for 'Sensemaya—Chant for Killing a
Snake' and 'Hunger'; Anne Wallace and New Canada Publica-
tions for 'Poem' by Anne Wallace; Harlan Howard and Bantam
Books Inc. for 'Busted' by Harlan Howard from *The Poetry of
Soul*; Daisy Myrie and Nelson Caribbean for 'Market Women'
by Daisy Myrie from *Ambakaila*; Slade Hopkinson for 'Electric
Eel Song'; Mervyn Morris and New Beacon Books Ltd for
'They' by Mervyn Morris; Eloise Crosby Culver and the
Associated Publishers Inc. for 'Harriet Tubman' by Eloise
Crosby Culver; Margaret Walker and Yale University Press for
'Lineage' by Margaret Walker from *For My People*; Barbara
Mahone and Harper & Row Publishers Inc. for 'sugarfields' by
Barbara Mahone from *The Poetry of Black America*; Maya
Angelou and Bantam Books Inc. for 'On Aging' by Maya
Angelou from *And Still I Rise*; Arun Kolatkar for 'Chaitanya'

142

and 'The Butterfly'; Deepak Kalha for 'Maths' and 'Conversations'; H.O. Nazareth for 'Reasons for Extinction'; Marc Matthews for 'The Friday Night Smell'.

Every effort has been made to trace all the copyright holders and the Publishers apologize if any inadvertent omission has been made.